Enriching the Immortal Soul

ENRICHING THE IMMORTAL SOUL

A Journey Towards God

TABITHA HENTON LAMB

CONTENTS

INTRODUCTION

This book is rich in the discourse of the soul. It explores the many elements that help enrich it, refine it, and discipline it in order to test it until it accomplishes its greatest goal: to bring pleasure to God.

What makes up the essence of a man is his spirit and soul. 1 Thessalonians 5:23 tells us that man is a three-part being composed of spirit, soul and body. The spirit of man, as expressed in the Hebrew word *ruach* in the Old Testament and the Greek word *pneuma* in the New Testament, is the divine part of man. The soul, *nephresh* in Hebrew or *psuche* in Greek, refers to man's intellect, emotions and will, which are deeply rooted in the spirit. It's the spirit that is the center of man and is able to connect with God in commanding the soul. The spirit should at all times be the driver of the soul, able to discipline and take charge of it, and not the other way around.

This book is about how the soul has to be nurtured and trained so that it lives at the best that God intended for it.

First, the soul must be trained through the exercise of patience, and this can only be achieved by enduring hard times through a true surrender. In patience, we learn to subdue the flesh, which is always seeking the greatest pleasure for itself.

The soul also embodies the human heart, which is the seat of all that we are. Proverbs 23:7 says: *"As a man thinketh in his heart, so is he."* Every action we take starts from the heart, so we must guard it carefully.

We also consider pain. As mature Christians, no matter the severity of the pain, we should view it as a tool to help us grow. Remember, ALL of the miracles in the Bible were for God's glory, but there was pain before those miracles took place!

Another factor that hinders the soul from truly experiencing fellowship with God is fear. Many of us have experienced pain, which could be severe in the case of trauma. Both experiences evoke fear. When we entertain fear, the soul remains faithless and weak until we surrender our hearts completely to the Holy Spirit.

Along the way, temptations are bound to afflict us What are temptations but cravings of our flesh which can range from simple pleasures to sinful lusts? If you overcome temptation, you'll be tried and tested. But your assurance is that temptations and trials are allowed by God so as to strengthen us.

Love creates the foundation for us to have more faith. If you truly love someone, there's no way you wouldn't trust them! It's the same with having faith in God, for God never fails and when it seems that He's quiet, He is working on something miraculous.

The stronger we abound in faith, the more we become eager to spend time with Him. Through consistent worship in His presence, we are filled with an overwhelming joy that cannot be earned through any other means but by constantly believing in Jesus and worshiping Him.

And, ultimately, we find the whole truth and are able to abide in it through His grace. The veil in our hearts is torn, and our soul is completely surrendered to the will of God.

Let's explore the workings of the soul in greater depth and learn how we can enrich it.

SPIRIT AND SOUL

"Spirit" and "soul" are often used interchangeably in the scriptures to denote the living breathing component of all animate life, separate from the physical component. The lasting or immortal parts of us are the spirit and soul. Together they make up the inner man with its feelings, its will, its knowledge, its intellect, its ability to connect with God and other spiritual powers. The soul feels and the spirit knows. Simply put, the human body is nothing more than a vehicle to house an invisible dynamic.

But spirit and soul are also distinct as we see 1 Thessalonians 5:23. Here Paul prays, *"I pray God your whole spirit and soul and body be preserved blameless unto the coming of our Lord Jesus Christ."* The spirit here is the invisible supernatural aspect of man, while the soul is the aspect which possesses appetites, mental faculties, feelings and emotions, desires and passions.

It is also important to know the distinction between the way animal life was formed and the way man was formed.

On day six, God simply spoke the animal kingdom into existence (Genesis 1:24): *"Let the earth bring forth the living creature after his kind, cattle, and creeping thing, and beast of the earth after his kind: and it was so."* But man was created in a totally different way. In Genesis 1:26 God says, *"Let us make man in our image, after our likeness"* and Genesis 2:7 tells us the Lord God formed man of the dust of the ground and breathed into his nostrils the breath of life.

In this way, man became a living soul. Note that, while man's body was formed out of the earth, his soul and spirit (the inner man) were created by the breath of God. We must note that breath does not come from within man. It comes from God, for it is the breath of life from God that causes body, soul and spirit to come together and function as a living whole.

Job 34:14-15 confirms this, affirming that we are nothing apart from God. We live and move and have our being because it is His breath and Spirit in us. When God decides to gather man's spirit and breath back to Himself, all flesh shall perish and man's body shall return to dust.

And so, God's breath brings vitality to the essence of man, his spirit, and his human soul. Interestingly, the Hebrew word for breath *ruach* is also the name for "spirit."

How do we keep our soul constantly alive through God's breath and looking to our Maker?

Command your Soul

t starts with a heart of gratitude:

Bless the LORD, O my soul, and all that is within me, bless His holy name. Bless the LORD, O my soul and forget not all His benefits. Who forgiveth all thine iniquities; who healeth all thy diseases; who redeemeth thy life from destruction; who crowneth thee with lovingkindness and tender mercies; who satisfies thy mouth with good things, so thy youth is renewed like the eagle's (Psalm 103:1-5).

So let's command our soul to bless the Lord who has saved us from destruction and to be grateful for all the good things He has given us. This sets us up for more blessing.

QUIETEN YOUR SOUL

My soul will wait on You, my Lord. It will trust in You. It will remain confident in You. It will hope in You. My soul will walk in obedience to You – Your will and Your Word. It will please You moment by moment, season by season. My soul, wait upon the Lord, be quieted within you and wait patiently for Him.

Surely I have behaved and quieted myself, as a child that is weaned of his mother: my soul is even as a weaned child (Psalm 131:2).

Quieted – is characterized by an absence of turbulence or disturbance, a peaceful calm. As a weaned child no longer cries, frets, and longs to be nursed, but is content and safe in its mother's bosom, so is my soul weaned from discontentment and is waiting for God. My soul waits in silence for God alone and quietly submits to Him. My hope is in Him.

Possess your Soul

In your patience possess ye your souls
(Luke 21:19).

n your patience, you will gain mastery of your soul. If you wait upon Him, He will redeem your soul from destruction. By continuing in patience, you will keep your soul in harmony with God. When your soul is in harmony with Him, you can command your soul to bless the Lord regardless of what life brings.

Many define patience as a delay in getting what we want. Most of us recognize that patience is one of the cardinal Christian virtues, but many of us are in no hurry to acquire it. Patience is not an option but is essential to the unity of the body of Christ. The Apostle Paul repeatedly commanded Christians to demonstrate patience (or longsuffering):

…walk worthy of the vocation wherewith ye are
called, With all lowliness and meekness, with
longsuffering, forbearing one another in love;

> *Endeavouring to keep the unity of the Spirit in*
> *the bond of peace"* (Ephesians 4:1-3).

First, we must understand that patience is both a command of God and a fruit of the Holy Spirit (Galatians 5:22-23). The Biblical portrayal of patience is not that of passive acquiescence but hopeful expectation, deeply rooted in our confidence in God's sovereignty and in His promise to show forth His glory in His perfect time.

Now besides patience, what else is required of us to enrich our soul?

A Death is Required

Not a physical death or one that brings sorrow or pain. On the contrary, it means the death of the "old man" within us when we die to our former sinful life. Bring born again is walking from death to life! And how do you know that you have entered the life of God which is promised to you? This only happens when the flesh is crucified; the old man is now dead and the new you is released. Once you do this, you'll be free from the curse of sin.

It's a paradox that the very weakness of our flesh is experienced in the strength of its sinful cravings and compulsions. It's maddening because our flesh frequently demands to think or do things that are the opposite of what we want to do or think at a given moment. These range from mildly distracting to disturbingly dark preoccupations. Consider these tendencies of ours:

- When, like the disciples, we should be watching and praying, our flesh wants to sleep.

- When we should be sleeping, our flesh can't get away from social media.

- When we should be diligently teaching our children as in Deuteronomy 6:7, our flesh prefers to watch the latest meaningless movie.

- When we should be meditating on scripture, our flesh instructs us to reorganize the living room, clean out the yard, or gossip about the political candidate.

- When we should be watching our diet, our flesh demands more comfort (unhealthy) food.

- When we should be basking in the joy and freedom of sexual purity and marital faithfulness, our flesh desires to indulge in watching porn on the internet.

These struggles made Paul the Apostle cry out, "*O wretched man that I am! who shall deliver me from the body of this death?*" (Romans 7:24). And if not for the grace of God towards us, our flesh would continue to hold us enslaved (Romans 6:20; Ephesians 2:3). Colossians 3:11 therefore encourages us to look upward for higher things: "*If ye then be risen with Christ, seek those things which are above, where Christ sitteth on the right hand of God.*"

Remember, he that loses his life for Christ's sake will gain it. The flesh must be crucified with the body of Christ. One must ask to be made over, and become a new creature in Christ. This includes the whole of man, where the Spirit gains mastery of the senses. This new man is equipped with a new heart and mind, with new desires, appetites, and deeds. Empowered by the Grace of God, and the Power to live a godly life here on earth, we take on His nature and His desires.

Unfortunately, when one determines to give up fleshly desires, there's usually a battle between one's mind and the former pleasures. It isn't a walk in the park. But it is something that must be done. Killing the flesh is completely subjecting it to the Spirit of God at work within you. You cannot destroy the desires of the flesh by your own self-will or effort. Like the wretched man in Paul's example, you'll fall right back into sin; only God can eventually pull you out.

But if the Lord Jesus killed the flesh, causing it to suffer by abstaining from food, and was able to overcome temptation, what does this tell us? It tells us that we too can surrender our addictions, weaknesses, sins, and evil habits to the Spirit of God – this is the crucifixion of the flesh. This kind of a death brings forth the new birth.

In Christ, God sets us free not only from the penalty of our sin, but also from the power of our sin that remains so active in our flesh (Romans 8:2; Romans 7:23).

The Word became flesh (John1:14). And so Jesus came in the form of human flesh so that He would be condemned in our place for our sin; in doing so He would pay the full penalty of our guilt. And then Jesus gives us His Spirit to empower us to walk in "newness of life" (Romans 6:4) so that we no longer are enslaved to the cravings and compulsions of our flesh (Galatians 5:16).

With the sin-penalty paid, we are free to receive His Spirit-power imparted to us, and walk in our kingdom inheritance (Matthew 25:34), all because our Father is so gracious and lavishly generous. What a gospel!

Let's now look at another way of describing man's inner self – through his heart.

The Human Heart

n the Old Testament, the Hebrew word *leb* is used to describe both the physical organ and the inner man: this is essentially his heart. This is close to the New Testament Greek word *kardia*, which also refers both to the physical heart as well as to its function as the seat and center of human life, hence his mind, soul, spirit, his entire emotional nature and understanding. As our control center, this implies a fusion of soul and spirit.

It is only through the love of God that the human heart can function at its highest capacity, that is, according to its original intent and design. Outside of this realm, one cannot know or trust the human heart. No outward obedience has value unless the heart turns to God. Left to its own devices, the heart is deceitful above all things, and desperately wicked: who can truly know it? God alone knows the heart. He searches it. He tries the reins for the purpose of distributing rewards according to the ways and doings of each man (Jeremiah 17:9-10).

The human heart is therefore one of the most significant elements in our Christian walk. The spiritual heart is seen from the very beginning when the Bible says we are made in the image and likeness of God (Genesis 1:26). God too has a heart, one that can be broken over our sins, a heart that we are encouraged by the life and ministry of Christ to follow.

It's this pursuit of the heart of God that God commends and seeks after. It was such a heart that got King David noticed by God.

The Lord said, *"I have found David the son of Jesse, a man after My own heart, which shall fulfil all my will"* (Acts 13:22).

In the same way, we are to be actively seeking the heart of God.

Again, Jesus emphasized cleanliness of heart when He told the Pharisees that only the thoughts that come out of the heart can make one unclean. Thoughts of pride, envy, lust, covetousness, deceitfulness all begin from one single thought, and if not controlled, can defile a person. One whose heart is prideful will seek ways to highlight their accomplishments. Some pivot to exaggeration to paint a perfect picture of themselves…and soon their hearts are filled with envy of others and plot to do anything to achieve their ambition.

In the wilderness, the children of Israel were led astray because of the wickedness in their hearts, and their refusal to repent. One must surrender the heart to the ruling of the Holy Spirit. Without this, the Spirit cannot enter. Jesus is knocking at the door of our hearts, waiting for an invitation to enter and through the Holy Spirit to guide our thoughts, sharpen our conscience and be our eternal guide (Revelation 3:20). This is the only way to gain righteousness.

The heart is also a region where love is tested and tried. We are commanded to show love to our fellow believers but sometimes we are overwhelmed by their behavior, motives or self-centered agenda, and we become hard hearted, bitter, angry and fail to forgive. God doesn't require hardness of heart, but a contrite and broken heart, one that is completely humble, remorseful and given to true worship (Psalm 51:17).

We know the heart is the starting place for spiritual life because of what the Bible says about God's actions towards the human heart. In order to for His people to desire what He desires, God must "*remove the heart of stone*" and replace it with "*a heart of flesh*" (Ezekiel 36:26). This is a humbling reality, and very difficult for many of us to accept. We want to believe that people, in their hearts, are essentially good and that they are coerced or victimized or provoked into bad behavior. But Jesus makes it clear that all manner of evil starts from the heart, and defiles the man:

> *For out of the heart proceed evil thoughts, murders, adulteries, fornications, thefts, false witness, blasphemies: These are the things which defile a man: but to eat with unwashen hands defileth not a man* (Matthew 15:19-20).

Many may wonder why King David was named a man after God's own heart given the atrocities he committed. David had been lured into sin because of his roving heart. He considered the beautiful woman, and then thought about how to satisfy the lusts of his thoughts! When he got her pregnant, he thought about a way to first attribute it to her husband and, when that did not work, to eliminate her husband so that he could marry the woman (2 Samuel 11:1-27).

His heart had been completely taken over by the devil.

But David's heart was eventually broken and he repented. He acknowledged his sins and his failure. There's nothing that pleases God more than a broken spirit and a contrite heart because He appreciates honesty (Psalm 51:17). Remember that God is a spirit, and they that worship Him must do so in spirit and in TRUTH! (John 4:24)

What can we learn about breaking the stony heart?

OVERRIDE SELF

To override self is to choose to love God more than oneself. It requires that we empty out our soul to allow God's life to flow through us. We are now in a right side up state once we are emptied of the false sense of being, until there is nothing of the defiling human flesh left. It is only then that life is right side up for mankind. We must decrease daily so the Spirit of God will increase.

Let us return to the original purpose of our creation, created for His good pleasure and not for the pleasure of a rebellious individual groomed by Satan. He did this when he deceived Eve in the garden. Since then, man has sought to carry out his own will and desires in what is essentially an act of rebellion. We must love our life to the death, so we can have true life. Why love ourselves to the point of eternal death and damnation when we can experience the greatest depth of love if we love ourselves to life?

Let us turn our hearts back to the God of our creation in the knowledge that He created all things and they belong to Him alone:

All things were made by him; and without him was not anything made that was made (John 1:3).

Thou art worthy, O Lord, to receive glory and honour and power: for thou hast created all things, and for thy pleasure they are and were created (Revelation 4:11).

Whatsoever is under the whole heaven is mine (Job 41:11).

But we have lived as if our lives are our own and convinced ourselves to stake a claim to this life as if we are indeed the author of our own destiny. We are moving alongside Lucifer, who has deceived himself to believe it is His universe. Let us return to God's purpose, and live our life as He originally designed and planned for man. This is what the Son of God made possible to all who would come to Him. But first, we must deny ourselves in absolute surrender to the One who holds all things together.

Colossians 1:16:

> *For by him were all things created, that are in heaven, and that are in earth, visible and invisible, whether they be thrones, or dominions, or principalities, or powers: all things were created by him, and for him...*

This leads us to our next discussion – the value of pain and trauma.

PAIN

We must first understand that pain is a tool in the hand of God. He allows it in our lives to purify, to change and to redefine us. It is the path to purpose. It brings growth, maturity and an awareness of things that are operating in us that we may be unaware of. If you trust the plan, you will trust the process.

> *For I know the thoughts that I think toward you, saith the LORD, thoughts of peace, and not of evil, to give you an expected end* (Jeremiah 29:11).

I want you to be the best you can possible be – from the heart of the All-Knowing, Sovereign and the only Omniscient One. He alone knows just the right friction or pressure to allow, and exactly how much of it to apply.

To those of us who are in Christ Jesus, everything must be driven out, including the curse on man due to the fall of

Adam, the works of the flesh, generational curses, works of darkness; sin, iniquity, fear and the sting of death.

When we know all things will work together for the overall good, we can trust the process. Neither happiness nor sadness nor how we choose to live our life can change this perspective on life.

We must also change how we view pain, for receiving the process it is just as good, if not more rewarding, than receiving happiness. How we receive it will cause a corresponding reaction in the soul of a man. When we view pain as something ultimately good for us, we will welcome it when it arrives. For it is a better friend to us than happiness. A person with this understanding will never reject what is most beneficial to his well-being. Our perspective will not change or falter because we know, regardless of the severity of the pain, that the end result will yield only all things working together for the good of them that love God, to those who are the called according to His purpose. This is the only possible outcome for those, whom with deliberate purpose He has called (Romans 8:28).

Understand that the tool He will use to get things in life that lie dormant until they are activated, is pain. When we trust Him completely, it allows us to move strategically with Him and not ignorantly against Him.

To move with His plan, through the process affirms our purpose. You may ask, what is purpose? Well, I am glad you asked. The original intent God still has in mind for mankind is to have pleasure in us as His creation.

Revelation 4:11: *…for thou hast created all things, and for thy pleasure they are and were created.*

Let us understand a little more about hurt. You see, hurt has a memory. It remembers what you said, what you did, or did not do, how if felt; it remembers every detail. But the only way to move forward is to position ourselves to forget. Paul in Philippians 3:13, revealed that path to us when he wrote,

> *Brethren, I count not myself to have apprehended: but this one thing I do, forgetting those things which are behind, and reaching forth unto those things which are before.*

In Isaiah 43:18, are we not commissioned to *"Remember ye not the former things, neither consider the things of old."* How can we receive the new if we purpose to keep remembering? We must renew our minds to do away with the old patterns in an effort to make way for the new. We must resolve to take on a new mind which is the mind of Christ. Only then are we guaranteed of peace.

There is an antidote for the soul just as there is an antidote for the physical body. You want to rid your life of trauma; redefine how you see pain. To a believer, pain is simply an agent in the hand of the Almighty God. If He allows pain in our life, we must trust and know it is for a definite purpose. There is good in it, or He would not have allowed it. Without pain, we cannot grow spiritually. God never promised us a pain-free life. But He did promise that when we pass through the fire, He will be with us (Isaiah 43:2). Jesus also said that we will face many trials and tribulations in life, but in Him we would find peace:

> *These things I have spoken unto you, that in me ye might have peace. In the world ye shall have tribulation: but be of good cheer; I have overcome the world* (John 16:33)

Without pain, we become stagnant, without growth. Sometimes God tests our faith in Him with pain. So many Christians have abandoned the Lord because things didn't go the way they expect. Such an attitude shows we were never truly in love with God, but simply wanted His benefits. How long can you stand with God if you are thrown off by a little discomfort?

Remember that nothing can ever separate us from the Love of Christ, not even pain (Romans 8:38-39). It is a mechanism that He uses to bring us to wholeness.

Let's take pain to another level and look at trauma.

TRAUMA

Which of us has not experienced trauma at some point in our lives? Trauma is the response to a deeply distressing or disturbing event, such as a car accident, rape or murder that simply overwhelms our ability to cope, and causes states of panic, depression, and helplessness that may last well past the event.

Victims of trauma are advised to seek professional help. But there is a limit to outside help. When we try to manage the trauma through our own resources, we limit the hand of God at work in our life. Yes, we can implement coping skills against the destructive impacts, better known as self-protect modes. But know that God did not design mankind as a whole to self-protect. Because we are limited in all areas of knowledge, we are often unaware of the destruction planned against our soul. Unless the Spirit of God is indwelling in us, we do not have proper access to the spirit world that is unseen to the human eye. We cannot hear any assuring voice because the voice of Trauma speaks out louder than the voice of God.

It is only when that voice is silenced that we can be free to be led by the Spirit of God. If we want to rid our life of trauma, we must redefine how we see pain. The recourse for trouble is to hasten to the throne of God. This is the only option; it is the only outcome for a believer in Christ. We know trouble will come, so let's redefine the process we use when it does. To put a new process in place, there should be a plan to respond to severe pain and not to react to it.

Do not allow hurt, pain, tragedies, the actions or lack of action of people, situations, or circumstances or disappointments to throw your life into trauma. We must not give people or circumstances that level of power or control over us, our happiness or well-being. This is where we have ceded control, authority and power of our life, its well-being and happiness into the hands of others.

What drives this behavior is the need for acceptance; but we must realize we have been accepted in the eyes of the one who matters most, and that is God. If we truly grasp this truth, the need of acceptance from others will diminish, and we can take back control of our destiny and place it in His hands. It is here we redefine this process and make an exchange: you give this devastating experience to God and Him alone, and He gives you His power.

Trauma forces us to build walls of self-protection. But those walls around our heart can crumble at a given moment with the next setback. We must bring Jesus into our focus, for has He not promised all that Labor that He will give us rest? He came to heal our mental and emotional pain. Psalm 147:3 says: *"He healeth the broken in heart, and bindeth up their wounds."* He came for the broken hearted, all who are bound, those who are captives of alcohol, addicts, sexually harassed and abused, wrongfully labeled, rejected and abandoned. All He wants is our surrender; it is here we can lay those fears at His feet.

Fear

When we walk in fear, it is because we are ignorant of the love of God, particularly in the area of trust. We may believe God is there for others but we do not believe God is there for us. To know and to experience His unconditional love gives us the courage to defeat fear. We must allow ourselves to experience His love. God will take care of us.

Do not make friends with fear. Speak the Word of God over your life immediately. Do not allow yourself to become afraid but claim you have the boldness of a lion. And be persistent in that claim. Being set free from something does not mean the disappearance of it. It will present itself. It does not mean we do not have to deal with the situation over and over again. It does mean, however, that we now have authority over that situation and can speak the Word of God over it.

Understand that fear is a demonic spirit and it does not come from God. *"For God hath not given us the spirit of fear; but of power, and of love, and of a sound mind"* (2 Timothy

1:7). Its sole purpose is to paralyze us and keep us from moving forward. Fear takes root when we allow it to control our lives. But God does not want us to be owned by fear.

Don't be driven by fear. It is not a battle for us to fight but it is God's. He allows circumstances as He did with Job, so we He can come to us in a way He has not come before. In order to destroy fear, we must take action. Any time fear enters the domain of our life, meaning, our heart, our mind or our mouth, know it did not come from God. Make a stand and pray against the spirit of fear. Instead of worrying, celebrate God in your life – all day, every day. Keep Him at the forefront of your mind.

> *Now the just shall live by faith: but if any man draw back, my soul shall have no pleasure in him* (Hebrews 10:38).

Remember that fear displeases God, while faith pleases Him. It makes us doubt that He is with us. But those who are bold and faithful please God because we believe that He is and is a rewarder of those who diligently seek him (Hebrews 11:6). Because He transcends time and space, and all earthly laws and human standards, He can do anything we ask of Him.

TEMPTATION

What is temptation? Temptation is a seduction into evil, a solicitation to do wrong. Temptation persuades us, deluding us it is good so that it may ruin us. Temptation moves stealthily by deception to lead us more or less unconsciously into sin. Think of temptation as the tempter looking through the keyhole into our private room, and sin as drawing back the bolt and making it possible for him to enter.

Let no man say – not if he is tempted (for temptation is certain) but *when* he is tempted – "God is tempting me." For God cannot be tempted with evil, neither does He tempt any man (James 1:13). Stop accusing God! Cease saying when you are tempted that God is at fault.

James tells us how we are tempted and gives us a strategy for overcoming the deadly lure of temptation: to overcome temptation we must first recognize its source, its force and its course. The lust of the flesh is the source which is evil in nature.

> *But every man is tempted, when he is drawn away of his own lust, and enticed. Then when lust hath conceived, it bringeth forth sin: and sin, when it is finished, bringeth forth death* (James 1:13-15).

James described this process of sin in four states, Desire, Deception, Disobedience and Death. Desire produces strong imagination, lust, delight in viewing. Deception causes lust to be conceived, and a yielding to sin. Disobedience leads to the sinful act committed, and, finally, Death is the consequence of actual sin.

Every man is tempted. We must stop being deceived regarding this strategic truth, lest we are swept downstream by the strong pull of the temptation that comes from within us. It is then only a matter of time when we are drawn away by our own lusts, and enticed. We are drawn away and enticed by what is already in our thought life. (To clarify further, no one else is to blame for this but me.) Then when what is in me (lust) has conceived, this particular lust brings forth sin: and sin, when it is finished, brings forth death, for the wages of sin is death.

Remember, temptation is not in itself a sin; in fact, to a believer, it is the call to battle. The point is we are in a continual war against our soul, and it is not simply a momentary skirmish. Our flesh, the evil world system and the evil one are resolutely determined to take us down to devour us!

Temptation is trying to get us to fulfill a desire (legitimate or illegitimate) in an illegitimate way out of the will of God. We may think of sin as a single act, but God sees it as an attitude. Adam committed one sinful act but that act reflected his inner rebellion, and it brought sin, death, and judgment on the earth and the whole human race.

If we feel we are not being tempted when we have a strong urge to do something, then chances are we are already deceived by the temptation and we don't even realize our dire state!

TRIALS/TESTINGS

Temptation can be distinguished from trials or testings. While temptation is a seduction to evil, trials or tests seek to discover the man's moral qualities or his character, to expose his limited capabilities. A test or trial is aimed at a man's good, making him conscious of his true moral self. God tries men but the motive of that trial is what differs from temptation. A temptation is of the devil to try to induce him to do wrong; but God tries men to test them that they may find out their weaknesses and be saved from doing wrong. He never causes a heart to be inclined towards evil. While He does all things, and is in all things, He, Himself does no evil, nor can He be charged for doing so.

Different kinds of trials may seem like an attack, but they are there to put to prove, examine and question our loyalty. Trials test our faith and the man who stands true in them proves his beliefs sound and his faith genuine.

James 1:1-4 says:

> *My brethren, count it all joy when ye fall into divers temptations; Knowing this, that the trying of your faith worketh patience. But let patience have her perfect work, that ye may be perfect and entire, wanting nothing.*

So testing works patience and patience works perfection, that is, personal perfection in the knowledge of the gospel and the will of God, and personal completeness in all the gifts of God. A test by implication reveals our trustworthiness, and what we are really made of.

TRUST

W hat are the characteristics of a man, who puts his trust in man, or his own abilities and whose heart is far from God?

Cursed be the man that trusteth in man, and maketh flesh his arm, and whose heart departeth from the LORD. For he shall be like the heath in the desert, and shall not see when good cometh; but shall inhabit the parched places in the wilderness, in a salt land and not inhabited (Jeremiah 17:5-6).

On the other hand, here is the man who puts his trust in God:

Blessed is the man that trusteth in the LORD, and whose hope the LORD is. For he shall be as a tree planted by the waters, and that spreadeth out her roots by the river, and shall not see when heat cometh, but her leaf shall be green; and shall not be careful in the year of drought, neither shall cease from yielding fruit (Jeremiah 17:7-8).

Again, Proverbs 3:5-6 tells us to trust God totally with all of our heart:

Trust in the LORD *with all thine heart; and lean not unto thine own understanding. In all thy ways acknowledge him, and he shall direct thy paths.*

Trust simply means to confide in, so as to be secure and without fear. It also implies to begin, to continue, and end every work, purpose, and plan with God. Unfortunately, self-sufficiency and self-confidence have been the ruin of man as he seeks to live independently and find his way in the world without God.

LOVE

The human heart is capable of human love but incapable of unconditional love. The only thing human love can guarantee is continuous heartbreak and pain. The maximum love it can give is love that is merited based on the highest degree of performance of the other. This love will never fail to disappoint. We must aim to experience the highest level of love – *agape* love – which is the purest kind of love because it is selfless. This is the unconditional, indwelling love of God, which He promises to put into our hearts.

1 Corinthians 13:4-7:

> *Love endures with patience and serenity, love is kind and thoughtful, and is not jealous or envious; love does not brag and is not proud or arrogant. It is not rude; it is not self-seeking; it is not provoked [nor overly sensitive and easily angered]; it does not take into account a wrong endured. It does not rejoice at injustice,*

but rejoices with the truth [when right and truth prevail]. Love bears all things [regardless of what comes], believes all things [looking for the best in each one], hopes all things [remaining steadfast during difficult times], endures all things [without weakening] (AMP).

Agape love is a spontaneous and divine love. It is a love that gives more than takes. We can see in 1 Corinthians 13:4-8, there are nine ingredients in this Divine Love that we can display:

- **Patience** – not demanding; shows kindness; bears, believes hopes, and endures all things (verse 4, 7)

- **Kindness** – love in action: never acts rashly or insolently; not inconsistent, puffed up, or proud (verse 4)

- **Generosity** – love in competition: not envious or jealous (verse 4)

- **Humility** – love in hiding: no parading; no airs; works then retires (verse 4)

- **Courtesy** – love in society: does not behave unseemly; always polite; at home with all classes; never rude or discourteous (verse 5)

- **Unselfishness** – love in essence: never selfish, sour, or bitter; seeks only the good of others; does not retaliate or seek revenge (verse 5)

- **Good temper** – love in disposition: never irritated; never resentful (verse 5)

- **Righteousness** – love in conduct: hates sin; never glad when others go wrong; always gladdened by goodness to others; always slow to expose; always eager to believe the best; always hopeful, always enduring (verses 6-7)

- **Sincerity** – love in profession: never boastful and conceited; not a hypocrite; always honest; leaves no impression but what is strictly true; never self-assertive; does not blaze out in passionate anger nor brood over wrongs, always just, joyful, and truthful; knows how to be silent; full of trust; always present (verse 8)

All of these traits display selfless acts of love. We must redefine how we see love according to the way Jesus the perfect Son of God modeled love. He came to love not to be loved. Even the world loves those who are good to them. But it takes a special love to love in darkness, to exercise love instead of hate. We love not only because a person is good, kind or deserving but because God wants the perfect love of the Son of God to be manifested in us so that His love can reach out to all.

He came to be to be hated, battered beyond recognition and brutally killed. He suffered in this way for all to see the perfect and unconditional love of God. Man has an opportunity to get it right because we are given a second chance. Why would He allow what He created in His image to be doomed or totally lost? He could not and He did not. He made provision for us, who were created in His image, to be redeemed.

FAITH

You may ask, what is Faith? Faith is the supernatural confidence and trust in God for the miraculous manifestation of His divine power. Faith is the underlying support for the ground work, the confidence needed for the unseen substance. It's the assurance of the reality pledged just as the title deed is the evidence of a property that is already your possession.

Hebrews 11:1 says: *"Now faith is the substance of things hope for, the evidence of things not seen."* The secret to pleasing God is approaching Him in faith, *"for without faith it is impossible to please Him: for he that cometh to God must first believe that He is, and that He is a rewarder of them that diligently seek Him"* (Hebrews 11:6).

Hebrews 11:3 talks of the invisible realm that came into being when it was called forth: *"Through faith we understand that the worlds were framed by the Word of God so that things which are seen were not made of things which do appear."* The ages were planned by the Word of God and the things that are now seen materialized by the spoken word.

What are the implications of faith in our prayers? If we wish to have our prayers answered we must ask in absolute unwavering faith, without doubting:

> *But let him ask in faith, nothing wavering. For he that wavereth is like a wave of the sea driven with the wind and tossed. For let not that man think that he shall receive any thing of the Lord. A double minded man is unstable in all his ways* (James 1:6-8).

For the man who has two minds, his only outcome is instability in all of his ways. A doubtful person is like a wave of the sea, rising in faith one moment, and sinking in hopelessness the next. One minute he believes; the next he does not. He says yes and then no to what God has promised, never making up his mind which way he believes. He staggers helplessly in prayer like a drunken man. A doubtful man will not get an answer. Only the man of faith will.

JOY

You may have heard about the nine fruit of the Spirit and wondered what they are and how they relate to enriching our soul. Here they are:

But the fruit of the Spirit is love, joy, peace, long-suffering, gentleness, goodness, faith, Meekness, temperance: against such there is no law (Galatians 5:22-23).

After love, the next fruit of the Spirit is joy. The word "joy" appears nearly 200 times in the Bible, showing how important this sweet fruit of the Spirit is.

Just as physical fruits require time to mature, the fruit of the Spirit will not ripen in our lives overnight. As we mature in our faith, all the characteristics of our spiritual fruit will grow as well.

People often confuse joy with happiness, but the two are not interchangeable. Joy is from within, regardless of what is going on around you. Happiness can be a fluctuating emotion, dependent on a situation, but joy is a constant enduring state of the heart. Joyful people make a commitment to gratitude regardless of the circumstances.

The most striking thing about joy is that you can find joy in adversity. That is exactly what James 1:2-4 encourages us to do:

> *My brethren, count it all joy when ye fall into divers temptations; Knowing this, that the trying of your faith worketh patience. But let patience have her perfect work, that ye may be perfect and entire, wanting nothing.*

This can be a difficult idea to grasp, because joy might be the last thing we are feeling when facing struggles. God knows our sorrows, heartaches and fears but He calls us to rejoice anyway because He wants us to be in joyful anticipation of His promises. *"Weeping may endure for a night, but joy cometh in the morning"* (Psalm 30:5).

In these difficult times, we may find our lives in a continuous process of dislocation and uncertainty, so that being joyful seems unnatural. Sometime we face adversity that is unprecedented. Certainly, many of us are not happy. But joy is an internal experience, and we can find joy in the midst of storms because of our faith in God's promises.

Through it all, know that the Joy of the Lord is our strength. The Joy He provides is a divine joy, gifted by God. This joy operates at a higher dimension, one that governs and has mastery over feelings, emotions and the human senses. If there is nothing to feel joyful about, think about Jesus' sacrifice on the cross with gratitude for the new lease of life we have been given.

How can the Holy Spirit the giver of joy increase our store of it? Through

- The Joy of salvation. Our greatest reason to be joyful is when God saves us from our destructions like the prodigal son (Luke 15:7).

- The Joy of God's presence. The Holy Spirit draws us to God in whose presence we can know true joy (Psalm 16:11).

- The Joy of spiritual maturity. As the Holy Spirit works in us to bear more fruit, we experience the joy of abiding in Him (John 15:11).

- The Joy of deliverance: When God sets us free from bondage, we rejoice like Hannah did when God delivered her from barrenness and blessed her with Samuel (1 Samuel 2:1).

GRACE

The grace of God is through and in His Son Jesus Christ. Jesus paid the price to reveal all of Heaven's resources to us to us and to make them available to us. Many times we misunderstand Grace. Grace is not an excuse to sin but rather the ability to overcome sin. What we cannot do in our own ability, Grace through Jesus Christ makes available the power to overcome all that weighs us down: sin and iniquity, the law, ordinances, death, and the works of the flesh. With Jesus we can fend off all demonic attack because Jesus came to destroy the work of the devil:

> *He that committeth sin is of the devil; for the devil sinneth from the beginning. For this purpose, the Son of God was manifested, that he might destroy the works of the devil (1 John 3:8).*

> *And you, being dead in your sins and the uncircumcision of your flesh, hath he quickened together with him, having forgiven you all*

trespasses; blotting out the handwriting of ordinances that was against us, which was contrary to us, and took it out of the way, nailing it to his cross; And having spoiled principalities and powers, he made a shew of them openly, triumphing over them in it (Colossians 2:13-15).

It was amazing Grace that transformed Persecutor Saul to Apostle Paul. It was Grace that emboldened the once timid Peter who denied Christ. It is Grace that moved Stephen to intercede for the very ones who were stoning him as he cried out, *"Lord, lay not this sin to their charge"* (Acts 7:60). Without Grace, we're nothing before God and with Grace we can do great exploits for Him. Let us come confidently before His throne and receive His Grace.

On the other hand, there are those who abuse the provision of Grace. These are false teachers and hard-hearted Christians. Slowly, the anti-Christ is creeping into the Church through falsified Grace teaching that grants people the license to live ungodly lives. Christians no longer appear different from the world, but seek to imitate every wrong move of the world. Instead of calling people who flaunt their ungodly lifestyles to order, we the church encourage them to take their time…and rebuke those that try to correct them.

> *For there are certain men crept in unawares,*
> *who were before of old ordained to this con-*
> *demnation, ungodly men, turning the grace*
> *of our God into lasciviousness, and denying*
> *the only Lord God, and our Lord Jesus Christ*
> (Jude 1:4).

Let us not misappropriate the Grace of God, for it is the power of God working in us and through us to carry out all of His will. In Him we have the ability and power to resist the enemy and he has to flee from us.

The first thing that Grace brings is transformation, the kind of change that only comes through supernatural intervention. Without our willingness to seek change in our behaviors and attitudes, we will not be appropriating Grace. We cannot receive the new wine in old wineskins.

Grace is light. When that change comes, you automatically become a light for others to follow. Anything outside it is darkness, and we can only have fellowship with the light of Grace if we walk in the light, just as Jesus did.

PEACE

The peace that Jesus gives to those who love Him guards the human mind, senses and emotions. It is not governed by thoughts, feelings or outcomes, but transcends all human understanding. The peace God gives is perfect. It cannot nor will it falter. We must never forfeit this peace or surrender it through deception, choosing to ground our thoughts in our experiences or what the world throws at us. When you do that, it's as much as saying: "I chose to give up the peace that God promises. I prefer the mental and emotional damage promised to me for operating outside of divine peace. I deem this more favorable or valuable than the gift of peace from God."

Peace is God's commitment to all those who meet the condition of keeping their mind stayed on Him, and who trust in Him at all times, in all things, and in all places:

Thou wilt keep him in perfect peace, whose mind is stayed on thee: because he trusteth in thee.

Trust ye in the Lord for ever: for in the Lord Jehovah is everlasting strength...” (Isaiah 26:3-4)

Spiritual peace doesn't mean an absence of problems. There may be untimely deaths, illnesses, miscarriages, losses of all kinds, financial problems, rejection, divorce and other crises; but we will still have an underlying sense of calm and confidence that all is well with our soul. This peace keeps us fixated on God even in the most tumultuous situations. Peace comes from FULLY trusting in God, and depending upon His word. It is the absence of anxiety and all forms of social pressure. Jesus understands the burdens that we carry as He Himself experienced the harshness of life as a man. This is why we are encouraged to cast our cares on Him, because He cares for us (1 Peter 5:7).

Peace then is the enduring quality of those who choose to live in hope and faith. Remember that our Lord is the Prince of Peace. He has broken every wall of division between men.

For he is our peace, who hath made both one (we and the others), and hath broken down

> *the middle wall of partition between us...*
> (Ephesians 2:14, emphasis added)

Finally, I want to talk about the veil that covers our hearts.

The Veil within My Heart

What can separate us from the love of God? According to Romans 8:38-39, nothing can. Only ourselves. It's the Veil within our hearts. A veil is a thing that serves to protect, to cover, to conceal, to disguise or to partition. The veil we are referring to is the heart which is resistant to the Spirit of the Lord.

This veil on our hearts is formed from our independent self life. It is made up of our self-concept, opinions, mindsets, thoughts, wisdom, feelings, intents and plans. This is our own conscience operating independently of the Holy Spirit dwelling in us.

The veil covered the hearts of the religious Jews in Jesus' day, and blocked them from receiving the gospel. They clung instead to legalism.

2 Corinthians 3:14-15:

> *But their minds were blinded: for until this day remaineth the same vail untaken away in the*

> *reading of the old testament; which vail is done*
> *away in Christ. But even unto this day, when*
> *Moses is read, the vail is upon their heart.*

Even when we have received Jesus and are born again, our resistance to the Holy Spirit with all His revelations, power, fruit and gifts causes dullness, bondage, and blindness. There is no radical change over time, no transformation into the image of Christ.

Sometimes we deliberately hold on to this veil by consciously hardening our hearts to the liberating effects of the gospel. If we are entangled by the pleasures and cares of this world, we cannot break out into the things above, and fail to understand that there are consequences for those who deliberately ignore the ways of God. At other times, the devil chooses to target us because of our shallow faith, inflicting us with doubt and confusion about the true message of God (Mark 4:1-20). Even when we desire the righteousness of Christ, the veil over our faces brings out our own self righteousness and prevents the light from penetrating our hearts.

When Apostle Paul was Saul the Pharisee, he had a covering over his face out of ignorance, arrogance and blind passion for the way that seemed right to him. But the encounter with Christ on the road to Damascus tore the veil, and set in motion a series of events that led to dramatic change. Ironically, it was only when his physical eyes were blinded that his spiritual eyes were open to the light (Acts 9).

For all those who are truly ignorant and are seeking, the Lord will show mercy and guide them to genuine ministers of the gospel. Think of how the Lord sent Philip the evangelist to the Ethiopian eunuch on the road to Gaza to deliver the message of salvation (Acts 8:26-40). On the other hand, for those who deliberately continue in their blindness and deny their inheritance, there is a price to pay. They fail to understand that there is a promise for those who **surrender** themselves, but not those who **continue** in fellowship with the devil. We are not to soft pedal such people for the sake of political correctness but warn them of their dire condition:

> *And others save with fear, pulling them out of the fire; hating even the garment spotted by the flesh* (Jude 1:23).

Once the veil has fallen from your eyes, you too have to help others see the Light. This explains why the Lord encouraged us to preach the Gospel of Jesus Christ, not just to our family or local church, but to the uttermost parts of the Earth.

The veil prevents us from seeing; it prevents us from knowing God's will; it prevents us from thinking, feeling and desiring the things that bring life. Removing the veil brings freedom from the law of sin and death, freedom from bondage, addiction, confusion and doubt, releasing us to conform to the image of Christ.

As our hearts become one with the Spirit, we will be transformed so that we reflect the person of Christ: we will think, feel and become more like Him. In short, we will have the mind of Christ (1 Corinthians 2:16). Our conscience will be changed – and we will be more sensitive to what does and does not please the Lord.

CONCLUSION

⁕

As I conclude this book, I would like to highlight the main truths we discussed, which are crucial to the safety and well being of our souls.

Our immortal souls should be our priority. Physical death does not end our life. As Jesus said in Matthew 10:28: *"And fear not them which kill the body, but are not able to kill the soul: but rather fear Him which is able to destroy both soul and body in hell."* Contrary to what many think, our final outcome after death is not dependent on our good works. It depends on our relationship with God through Jesus Christ and the good works that He leads us to (Ephesians 2:8-10).

Therefore, we must Command the Soul, that is, take charge of it and position it to have the right posture towards God. We must quieten and calm the soul to bring it to maturity through the exercise of patience. This will require a certain kind of death – a denial to self, the process of emptying our self life to receive God's life. This is often experienced with pain; but we will come to recognize that pain is an agent in the hand of God, a tool, if you will, for our healing and strengthening.

The pain and trauma we experience often lead to fear. Entertaining fear causes the soul to be faithless and weak. However, as mature Christians, we should regard pain, no matter the degree, as a tool to help us grow. Without challenges, we will not know our ability to stand in faith and hope in God, and the glory of God, in turn, cannot be fully manifested in our lives. There's nothing we can do in this state except to surrender our hearts completely to the Holy Spirit.

Even if we learn to deal with pain, temptations will come our way. We overcome temptation by acknowledging that temptations and trials are allowed by God to strengthen our soul. The difference between temptations and trails is that temptations are of the devil to beguile and to lure, and trial or tests are of God. We now accept these trials because we now trust the process at work in our lives.

This brings to an absolute trust in the Sovereignty of God. When we understand that God is in control, we also learn to trust Him completely because He has the final say in all our circumstances.

Love lays the foundation for us to have more faith. If you truly love someone, there's no way you wouldn't trust them!

What more God, who never fails! When it seems He is quiet, He is about to break through.

The stronger we abound in faith, the more eager we become to spend time with Him in consistent worship and fellowship. As we learn to enter into His Presence and enjoy the Lord, joy fills our being.

Once we know the truth about Grace and the proper function of Grace, we learn to live above sin, supernaturally equipped for every good work God calls us to do.

This brings us to the final section of this book: the Veil of My Heart. We can choose whether the veil will either be rent or remain intact and separate us from a true revelation of Jesus. The battle will be won or lost here. Once the veil is removed, our souls can bask in Divine peace. What can hinder a truer experience of the Affairs of the Soul?

My brothers and sisters, it is my prayer these tools can be used for your victory here on earth and your heavenly citizenship. Use these tools well and your tenure on earth will have good success and your eternal state will be assured.

> *He hath made every thing beautiful in his time:*
> *also he hath set the world in their heart, so that*
> *no man can find out the work that God maketh*
> *from the beginning to the end* (Ecclesiastes 3:11).

Made in the USA
Monee, IL
07 July 2026

56553669R00066